Old COLINTON

by
Peter Gray

C000264406

£2.99 W46

© Peter Gray 1999
First published in the United Kingdom, 1999,
by Stenlake Publishing, Ochiltree Sawmill, The Lade,
Ochiltree, Ayrshire, KA18 2NX
Telephone / Fax: 01290 423114

ISBN 1 84033 083 X

THE PUBLISHERS REGRET THAT THEY CANNOT SUPPLY
COPIES OF ANY PICTURES FEATURED IN THIS BOOK.

FURTHER READING

The books listed below were used by the author during his research. None of them are available from Stenlake Publishing. Those interested in finding out more are advised to contact their local bookshop or reference library.

The Balerno Branch, Donald Shaw, Oakwood Press, 1989.
Colinton – Seven Walks, Colinton Amenity Association, 1985.
A Water of Leith Walk, John Tweedie.
The Colinton Story, Lynne Gladstone-Miller, St Andrew Press, 1994.
Villages of Edinburgh, Malcolm Cant, John Donald, 1987.

ACKNOWLEDGEMENTS

Without doubt my deepest and sincerest thanks go to my wife Sharon – without her help and encouragement this book would never have been started, let alone finished. Thanks also to my daughters Sarah and Alison for their technical advice and help. Finally to all my friends, not only for their extreme patience while I searched for new material, and their assistance in finding new postcards, but also for their exhortations!

The Covenanters Monument is a thirty-foot high cluster of four Ionic columns which once formed the colonnade in front of William Adam's Edinburgh Royal Infirmary, demolished in 1884. The monument was erected and paid for by Mr R. A. Macfie, owner of Dreghorn Castle, *c*.1885.

INTRODUCTION

The character of present day Colinton has been forged and shaped by centuries of history. Celtic clans once hunted in the vicinity; Romans marched to and from their camp at nearby Comiston; Cromwellian raids took place; the village was romanticised by Robert Louis Stevenson; was plundered by highwaymen; and remains today as a village suburb of Scotland's capital. The Water of Leith has flown continuously through all these events, a source of power for the mills that were built along its banks, and hence an important source of employment.

Colinton originated as a small group of simple turf dwellings, thatched with reeds from Redhall Bog or Bonaly Burn, clustered in the sheltered valley through which the Water of Leith flows. The village grew around the ancient church of Halis (or Hailes) situated by the ford on the river.

The ford was the reason that Colinton (originally called Hailes) became established in the first place. Up to the mid-nineteenth century this ford lay on the route from Melrose to Dunfermline Abbeys via the Queen's Ferry on the Forth. These abbeys were two of the most important in Scotland. The Long Steps, next to what is now John Menzies in Bridge Road, follow the original route to the ford from the Pentland Hills.

The arrival of the Norman barons saw the introduction of the feudal system to the lands of Hailes and Redhall. Of these barons, perhaps the most important and influential was James Foulis, who acquired land all over the parish and established himself at Colinton Castle, a splendid building both in terms of defence and amenity. The ruins of the castle can be seen within the grounds of what is now Merchiston Castle school (the school takes its name from Merchiston Castle at Bruntsfield where it was housed until the 1930s).

In 1540 a crown charter was granted by James V which incorporated all the lands of the Foulis family into the Barony of Colinton. Just over a hundred years later, in August 1650, a column of Roundheads stormed the village, ransacked it, and at the same time burned and vandalised Colinton Castle. The ransacking was the Roundheads' revenge on the Royalist barons of Colinton and Redhall. The Foulis family continued to live at Colinton, but their fortunes never recovered from their uncompromising stand against Cromwell. The castle was sold off to pay the family's debts in 1801 after the estate had been disposed of piecemeal. Sir William Forbes, a successful banker, bought the castle.

With the decline of the feudal system, new houses were gradually built in the vicinity of Colinton by Edinburgh's rich merchants and burgesses. Retaining their cramped townhouses in the closes of the High Street for the winter months, they moved to the green spaces of the country in summer, using coaches and riding horses to travel to their places of work. The commuter age had arrived!

Like similar peripheral rural communities, the lifestyle of those who lived in Colinton was barely affected by the City of Edinburgh up until the middle of the nineteenth century. However, with the development of the railway and other forms of public transport, considerable expansion took place towards the end of the century, particularly around Woodhall Road and Spylawbank Road. Before the advent of the railway (which was opened in 1874), Colinton was the smallest of the villages on the Water of Leith, made up of a cluster of cottages around the ancient bridge. The railway opened up the area, although it was not met with universal approval, especially by the heritors of the parish church. A young engineer – William Arrol – worked on the new line, prior to beginning his most important venture, the Forth Railway Bridge. Access to the station, which was difficult from the old bridge, was by a new bridge that spanned the Water of Leith and the railway line, and provided an access road to the station. With the opening of the railway gradually more gentlemen moved to the village where they built their villas.

Widespread bungalow development occurred prior to the Second World War, and in the last few decades the style of housing has become even more varied. Despite the rapid growth around it, the old village has remained the focal point of the community.

Colinton is an area with an unusually high number of old houses and castles, the original owners of which took responsibility for the maintenance of the church, manse and school. These houses still provide a tangible link with the village's earlier history. The south side of Spylaw Street is almost completely taken up by a low row of pantiled cottages with timber porches over the pavement. These cottages, originally owned by James Gillespie, snuff-maker, were mill-workers cottages and may have been built for employees at Gillespie's snuff mill. In recent years they have been renovated under the direction of the Merchant Company Endowments Trust. Other houses were built in the village for wealthy members of Edinburgh society, and these have left Colinton the legacy of the finest group of early buildings designed by Sir Robert Lorimer. There are also splendid examples of the work of Sir Robert Anderson.

Colinton Village is still linked to Edinburgh by its own road. From 1751 onwards The Wrights Houses Turnpike Trust managed Colinton Road, and travellers to and from the village paid their tolls at the toll bar set up near Tollcross. This continued until the abolition of the turnpike system in 1882. Many of the existing roads in Colinton follow the old packhorse trails to the ford, and as a result are narrow and unsuitable for modern traffic. In 1979 work began on the Colinton section of the Edinburgh City Bypass, and this was completed in May 1981 at a cost of £12m. The bypass has succeeded in diverting traffic from the congested village, but has resulted in the constant noise of cars and the possibility of more houses being built up to the edge of the new road.

The Sixpenny Tree, at the foot of Redford Road, was a well-known landmark in Colinton, although due to disease the original tree had to be removed and a sapling now stands in its place. Many explanations have been given as to the origins of the name. The one claiming greatest authenticity states that the tree marked the approximate meeting place of the members of the Guild of Papermakers. It is said that guild members from the mills on the Water of Leith and the Esk Valley met there to debate the important issues of the day, and to pay their guild dues of sixpence into the coffers. It should be borne in mind that it was along way from the Esk to Colinton and the Colinton Inn was near to the tree!

In 1909 Colinton Tramway Co. planned to construct an electric tramway from Colinton to the cable tram terminus at Craiglockhart. The main impetus for this project was the proposed Redford Barracks, which the War Department was about to build to the east of Colinton. The tramway was never completed, however, and in 1920 Edinburgh Corporation acquired the Colinton Tramway Co. (which existed in name only). Trams finally arrived in Colinton in 1936, being preceded by the first local bus service which operated between 1920 and 1926.

Two years after the end of the First World War Colinton became an Edinburgh suburb and life changed dramatically. Fewer people worked in the community, the number of farm jobs decreased, residents began to do more of their shopping in town, and the mills ceased to flourish.

Colinton was designated a Conservation Area on 14 July 1977. By the end of the 1980s most of the major houses had ceased to be private residences. Colinton House had become the science block of Merchiston Castle school, Redhall House was part of the Graysmill School complex, and Hailes House was being used as offices. Redford House, Spylaw House and Bonaly Tower had all been converted to flats. A wing was added to Woodhall House to accommodate Jesuit priests, and the building has since been converted to flats. Modern dwellings now stand on the site of West Colinton House. Woodfield House, previously occupied by the Nuns of the Convent of The Good Shepherd, is now a modern housing development. Mackenzie's Cottage, the former home of Henry Mackenzie, author of *The Man of Feeling* and *The Man of the World*, is now an architects office.

The Pentland Hills form an imposing southern backdrop to Colinton, with easy access via Bonaly Road to the hills and the wonderful views that they offer of Edinburgh and beyond. With its rural character, wooded riverside walks, and extensive history, the village provides first class surroundings for those that live there.

Colinton Dell is a haven of peace and quiet in the midst of the thriving city suburbs – but it was not always as tranquil. The Water of Leith was one of the most industrialised rivers in Scotland, supporting around eighty mills on ten miles of water. Robert Louis Stevenson said of the scene that it was characterised by 'the sound of water everywhere and the sound of mills'. When the picture was taken the stepping stones were the only means of crossing the water. This rather precarious method has been made unnecessary by the construction of a rustic bridge.

Mills along the Water of Leith most commonly produced flour, snuff and paper. There are records of a paper mill at Spylaw in 1682 and a snuff mill at East Mills in 1749. The Bank of Scotland had its twenty shilling banknote manufactured at Boag's Mill in 1735. By 1769 the paper for the bank notes was being made at Redhall Mill (above). Although originally water-driven, the mills later converted to coal-fired production, and thrived with rail development which made cheap coal readily available. The only mill still in existence on the Water of Leith is Inglis Grain Mill, and that is used for grain-drying rather than actual milling. The man-made weirs and falls which were built to increase the force of the water for the mills can still be seen throughout Colinton Dell.

The only remaining evidence of the snuff mill at East Mill (right) is the weir and lade outflow. It was built high on the south bank of the Water of Leith with part of its structure protruding dangerously on timber supports towards the river. Mills were often constructed from wood, and this made them vulnerable to fires. In 1867 Boag's Mill was destroyed by fire and in 1890 Kates Mill (records of which date back to 1540) suffered the same fate. The small wooden pedestrian bridge linked the snuff mill with the grain mill on the opposite bank.

Another view of the snuff mill site at East Mill. The mill house, situated to the left, has survived. The low buildings on the right are the steadings of Wylies Farm, which provided ponies for local gala days and theatrical events in Edinburgh.

The original Mossy Mill is thought to have dated from the sixteenth century when it was a waulk mill, owned by the brothers Mosie from which the modern name is derived. Waulk mills were used for beetling cloth – beating it to make it flatter and finer. Mossy Mill was converted to a paper mill in 1838. The high square chimneys seen in the picture have since disappeared, and the mill is unfortunately now largely derelict and about to be demolished to provide housing land. The weir and lade that served it are in almost perfect condition, and the entrance sluice, relief sluice and gate can still be seen. Mossy House, the imposing former residence of the mill owner, is situated above the mill.

This photograph of Heather Cottage on Edinburgh Road, taken *c*.1910, shows Mrs Dickson, the wife of Jock Dickson the local chimney sweep, at her doorway. The cottage was built as a lodge for Colinton House and until 1900 still had an earth floor and thatched roof. It was a typical 'but and ben' design with the door in the middle of the front wall. The chimney was built on the gable end of the house to stop the thatch from catching fire.

This picture is thought to show the Gala Day procession in Colinton Village, with the procession passing Heather Cottage. Little is known about this event, which has not survived the passage of time. The stone pillars on the left mark the entrance to the Episcopal Church.

An early picture showing pupils heading towards the ashlar faced school building in the middle of the picture. The history of the local school can be traced back to 1651 when rudimentary accommodation was provided beside the parish church. Unfortunately the first headmaster was dismissed in 1655 for brewing and selling drink in the schoolhouse. The school provided an education not only for children of the middle and lower ranks, but also for many gentlemen. By 1811 the old thatched school and schoolhouse that stood near the manse gate was beyond repair and the Kirk Session instructed that a new schoolhouse should be built to accommodate 120 scholars in the upper village. The school moved in 1815. An inscription over the door of the old school by the manse translated as 'Either Learn, Teach or Go Away'.

Looking towards Colinton from the main Edinburgh road. The school building of 1815, obscured by trees in this picture, went on to serve as a library, doctors' surgery and private house. In 1843 a Mr Hunter was employed at a salary of £34 – plus £40 in fees – to teach 100 pupils English, writing, geometry, arithmetic and geography. This was in addition to his duties as session clerk, clerk to the heritors, postmaster and collector of parochial assessments.

Structurally, little has changed since this postcard was produced. The Colinton Inn continues to trade, but Rangecroft the fishmongers has long since disappeared.

The main road through Colinton has changed very little since this picture was taken *circa* 1910, although the amount of traffic has increased considerably. The pestle and mortar sign above Baillie the chemists disappeared when the shop moved to its present location in the centre of the village. The shops to the left, with houses above, were built and named 'Janefield' by the postmistress of Colinton, Mrs Johnstone.

The junction of Bridge Road and Spylaw Street at the beginning of the nineteenth century, showing the cottage and garden which stood on this site before the bank was built *circa* 1908. Spylaw Street leads down to the old ford and parish church. The chimney-stack of one of the old mills stands at the bottom of the road. In 1792 the Water of Leith provided water for 24 flour mills; 14 oatmeal mills; 12 barley mills; 7 sawmills; 6 snuff mills; 5 cloth fulling mills; 4 paper mills; 2 lint mills; and 2 leather mills. The chimney of the board mill is visible at the bottom of the street.

The inn at the top of Spylaw Street, close to its junction with Bridge Road at the gates to Spylaw Park, provided convenient refreshment for travellers. Formerly the Railway Inn, it has since been renamed the Royal Scot.

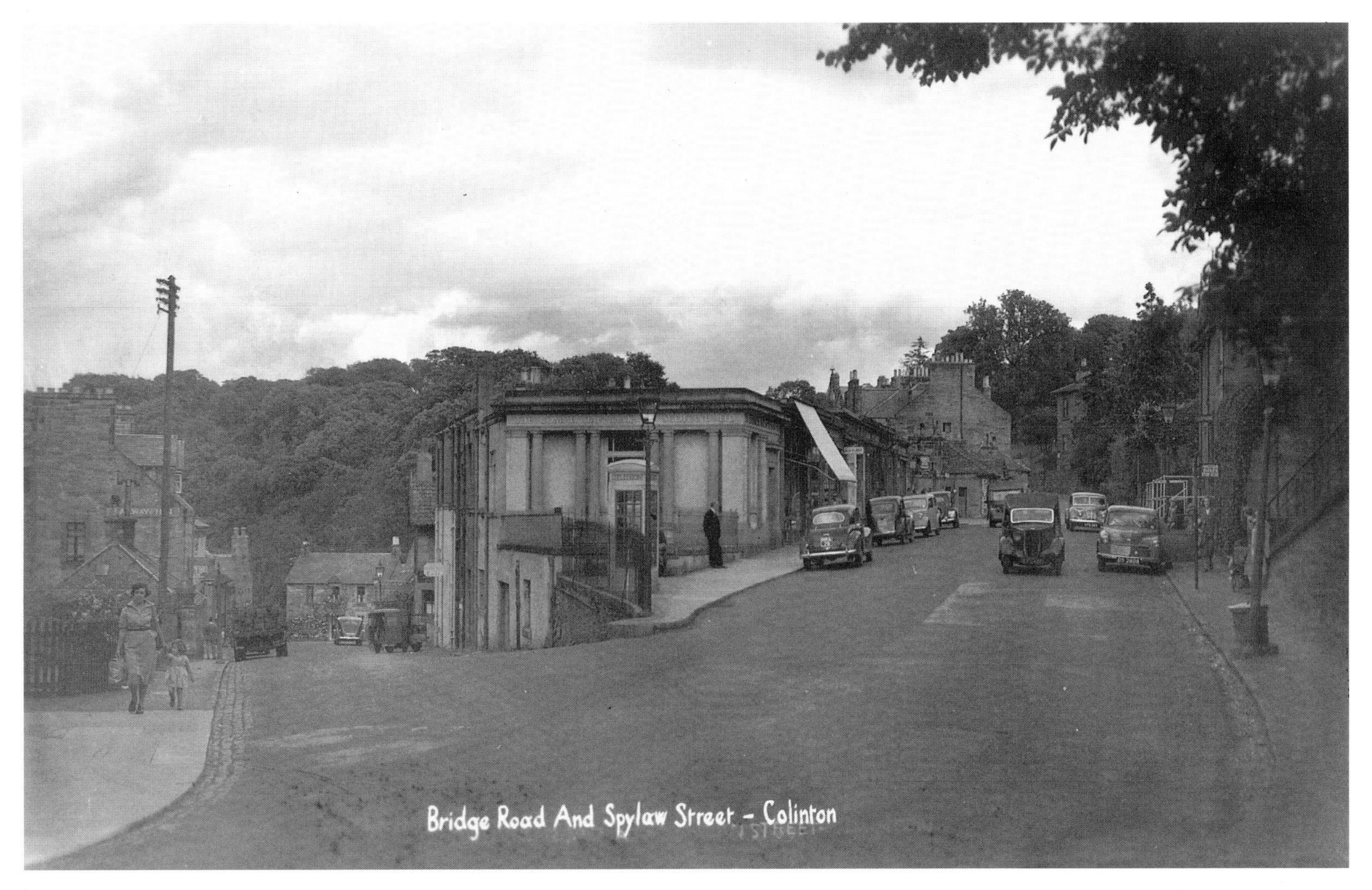

The junction of Bridge Road and Spylaw Street remains almost the same today as it did in the early 1950s. The bank continues to operate although the building has since been renovated.

A view down Spylaw Street from Cuddies Lane, looking towards the old ford, single arch bridge and the parish church. The Railway Inn is on the left, although the railway ran some way behind the inn and across the water. In April 1776 there was a customs raid on Upper Spylaw Mill where it was reported that the top storey was being used by smugglers. The raid uncovered three anchors of brandy and 2,500 pounds of tea.

The pantiled cottages on the left of this picture of Spylaw Street were originally occupied by mill workers. The Merchant Company of Edinburgh acquired them in 1799 under the will of James Gillespie. Although they have been modernised, their character (and unusual porches) remain intact.

This view of the old village was taken from the single arch bridge across the Water of Leith which replaced the ford. The Long Steps are in the middle of the picture. At the very top of these steps is the Colinton Inn. It is believed that the building immediately to the right of the steps, at the bottom, was the registrar's office and post office.

This picture, *circa* 1910, was taken from the station-master's cottage at the top of Kirk Brae (also known as Hailes Brae). Kirk Brae was a steep road leading from the church. Large stones were placed at the roadside on the brae to allow dray carts to rest their horses while negotiating the hill. The substantial villas of Woodhall Road are in the background; the pantiled cottages visible through the gap in the foreground are those which were acquired by the Merchant Company of Edinburgh in 1799. In the centre are the Long Steps, which took travellers from the Pentland Hills to the ford and the church.

This narrow bridge once formed the main route through Colinton. The station lay to the left in the dell, with Spylaw Park to the right. The imposing villas on the hill stand in Woodhall Road. The bridge has now been widened by cantilevers on either side to cope with the increased volume of traffic.

Colinton Bridge with the coal house, the office of the local coal merchant, visible to the right on the far side of the bridge. The office was situated at the top of the road leading to the station and goods yard. The steps in the left foreground lead to Spylaw Park (sharp right) and Woodhall Road (straight ahead). The path to Woodhall Road is known as The Twirlies and provided a shortcut to the station. At the top of this path was a lane to Bonaly known as The Witches Walk. The former Trustee Savings Bank building (now occupied by the Pentland Conservative Association) was originally built as shops. Mrs Andrew Neil's house was situated above the shops, and Colinton's first telephone exchange was housed in its large front room.

Colinton Bridge from Gillespie Road showing the railway line on its approach to the station on the far side of the bridge. Beyond the station was the tunnel that cut through the hill to Kingsknowe station. Jacob's Ladder, the steps from the station to the station-master's cottage, are visible left of centre above the bridge. The area in the left foreground was part of Downe's Nursery, which supplied produce to their shop in the village.

The Water of Leith, seen from what is now the site of a bridge on the City Bypass. In the centre is the old Balerno branch line, initially operated by the Caledonian Railway Company. Although called a branch line, it was in fact a loop, since the spur ran west from Balerno before rejoining the main Caledonian Railway line between Glasgow and Edinburgh. Following an accident in 1880, the line was described by a Board of Trade officer as 'a single line of bad curves and gradients'. The bridge in the foreground leads to Mossy Mill; the steeply sloping bridge in the background, which led down to Upper Spylaw Mill, is now derelict.

The railway line that served Colinton was opened on 1 August 1874. Although mainly intended to convey goods traffic to and from the many mills on the upper Water of Leith, a passenger service was provided from the outset. It was the first of the Caledonian Railway's local lines to carry passenger traffic. Passenger services were withdrawn on Saturday 30 October 1943 – the final train was the 20.19 service to Edinburgh, carrying 24 passengers. Freight services continued until 4 December 1967. The coal wagons in this picture of the station belonged to local coal merchant Hastie's (a coal cart can be seen between the wagons and the shed). Jacob's Ladder, the path at the east end of the station, led to the station-master's house at the top of the hill.

This picture, with a passenger train at the station, was probably taken from the top of Jacob's Ladder. The tunnel at Colinton cost £2,400 and the station £447.17s. Perhaps the best-known station-master was Mr John Kerr, who lived in the cottage that went with the job from 1874, and was well-known for his loud voice and hot temper. In 1973 this formerly busy railway line was converted to the Water of Leith Walkway.

Juniper Green station, with the footbridge over the Water of Leith in the foreground. Unlike Colinton station, which lay across the river from the village and out of sight behind trees, Juniper Green station lay directly below the main village street. Juniper Green station was closed on 11 August 1958, and Woodhall Paper Mill subsequently used some of the old station buildings.

Present-day commuters will appreciate this tranquil scene showing the Gillespie Crossroads before the vast developments at Wester Hailes, Currie and Balerno. The small track to the right is now the main road from Colinton to Wester Hailes and beyond.

A stone bearing the date 1636, salvaged from an earlier manse, is set into the wall of the building in the picture. This manse dates from 1784 and was built by Robert Weir (mason) and Thomas Jack (wright). One minister, Dr John Walker, wasn't satisfied with the building, and complained about the 'very insufficient workmanship'. The complaints continued until the heritors wearily agreed to repairs costing £37! Further additions were made to the house in 1807. Colinton's most famous minister was probably Dr Lewis Balfour, maternal grandfather of Robert Louis Stevenson. Stevenson described the manse as a 'well loved house, its image fondly dwelt upon by many travellers'. In *Kidnapped* Stevenson alludes to the manse and the old yew tree in its grounds. Throughout his book *A Child's Garden of Verse* there are many references to the manse, gardens and the area of Colinton.

The ancient church of Hailes (Hailes being Colinton's old name) is thought to have been established around 1095. It was dedicated to St Cuthbert, who was born in 635 and started life as a shepherd boy in the Lammermuir hills. He went on to train at Melrose, became Bishop of Lindisfarne, and died in 687. There are records of a church at Hailes being dedicated on 27 September 1248, and it is known that a new church building was constructed in 1636. In 1666, the night before the Battle of Rullion Green, the churchyard was used by Covenanters as a camp because the site could easily be defended.

In 1771 a new church was built by Robert Weir (mason) and William Watters (wright), to their own design. The architect David Bryce made changes to the building in 1837. Substantial alterations were carried out in 1908 by Sydney Mitchell, who repositioned Bryce's square tower over a new entrance porch (the previous picture shows the old design of the church, before Mitchell's alterations). The oldest surviving tombstone is a mural tablet dated 1593, although unfortunately many of the gravestones have suffered badly from the elements. Inside the entrance to the churchyard stands an old mort safe, weighing around 1,000 kilograms. At one stage there were six such safes. These were used at the time of the resurrectionists to prevent newly-buried bodies from being stolen for medical research. On occasion armed villagers took it in turns to guard the graveyard.

A rear view of the pre-1908 parish church looking towards the village and the Pentlands. The footpath to the right leads to Colinton Dell. At the far left, in very close proximity to the church and occupying part of the cemetery ground, is Kirkland Board Mill. Its proximity to the church led to numerous complaints about noise and dust. Kirkland Mill was destroyed in 1916 following a serious fire.

The Episcopal Church was designed by Sir Robert Rowand Anderson, a resident of Colinton. Following six years of campaigning and fund-raising, work on the building began in 1888. This was made possible by a substantial grant from the Walker Trust. A nominal feu duty of a peppercorn was levied. The church was opened on 10 August 1889 by Bishop Dowden, but it was 20 July 1893 before it was consecrated. Between 1893 and 1898 large-scale alterations were made because the church was proving too small. A south transept, organ-chamber and tower were added in 1895. In 1930 further additions comprising a new porch, baptistry and choir vestry were made, and the nave was also extended. Today the church is surrounded by attractive landscaped policies. Stained glass windows, a carved oak lectern and memorial pews are all features of this listed building.

The Convent of the Good Shepherd was situated between the Water of Leith and the foothills of the Pentlands. Its grounds originally stretched from what is now Woodhall Road down towards the Water of Leith. Apart from being home to an order of nuns, the convent was also used as a school, and a temporary home for Vietnamese boat people. The grounds were sold for private housing, and the convent building was demolished during development in the 1980s.

The starting point of the annual Sunday school trip has always been the church hall in Dreghorn Loan (the Loan Hall). This picture shows the gathering for the 1908 or 1909 trip, with the Loan Hall, the social centre of the village, in the background. The destination was often the polo field or a local park. Present-day trips venture further afield.

Because of the expansion of the parish at Colinton an iron church (so-called because it was made of corrugated iron) was established at Craiglockhart in 1880. This was later moved to Juniper Green where it also served as an overspill church. The building finally became Colinton church hall, affectionately known as the 'tin hall', located in Dreghorn Loan. In 1925 a campaign was launched to raise money to replace the tin hall. The fund got underway with £65 from the sale of the old iron building. This picture is thought to show the cast of a drama production given by the Colinton Literary Society. The show took place in the Loan Hall, and one of the cast has written: 'This is a sad sight. When the flashlight went off I got such a shock I went all goggly! The show went off quite well'.

Spylaw House, built in 1773 by James Gillespie, was situated in front of a building dating from 1650 in which Gillespie established his snuff factory. Frugal and industrious, Gillespie amassed great wealth from the business. He died on 8 April 1797 and his vast fortune was left for the endowment of a hospital and a free school for poor boys – James Gillespie's School. In 1940 the house became a youth hostel and then the regional headquarters of the Boy Scouts Association. It is now a listed building, surrounded by majestic old chestnut, maple and ornamental trees, and has recently been converted into private flats.

Colinton House was commissioned by Sir William Forbes (a banker friend of Sir Walter Scott) in 1801, although he died in 1806 before he could inhabit it. It was once the home of Lord Abercromby, a Speaker of the House of Commons. The house now forms part of Merchiston Castle School. Its grounds originally extended to Colinton Dell, and the ice-house which was used for the storage of ice for preserving food can still be seen there.

Colinton Cottage (substantially bigger than the average modern 'cottage'), is situated on the corner of Pentland Avenue and Gillespie Road, overlooking the Water of Leith. It was the first of several houses to be built in Colinton by Sir Robert Lorimer (1864-1929). As an architect, Lorimer was particularly associated with the restoration of castles, and also designed the Scottish National War Memorial (1928) in Edinburgh Castle.

The cottage was originally built for Sir Robert Lorimer's aunt, Miss Guthrie Wright, and later became a rest home for Queen's Nurses. It was described by one of the nurses as being 'as comfortable as it is pretty'. This picture shows the drawing room.

The name Dreghorn is ancient, and appears in a crown charter of Robert II (King of Scotland, 1371-1390). The original Dreghorn Castle was probably built by Sir William Murray, Master of Works to Charles II. One Alec Trotter bought the castle in 1799 and proceeded to enlarge and lavishly refurbish it. In 1881 it was visited by the King of Hawaii who came to see its then owner, Mr R. Macfie, who had a major interest in a sugar plantation in Hawaii. (As a result of this visit Robert Louis Stevenson met King Kalakaua in Hawaii in 1889.) Dreghorn Castle stood within the lands now occupied by Dreghorn Barracks. By the 1950s the castle – which had had a varied history, including a spell as a boys prep school – had fallen into disrepair. Poor maintenance, dry rot and vandalism necessitated its demolition. In the autumn of 1955 it was set on fire in a fire service exercise, and the following Sunday it was blown up by the army in a TA exercise. All that remains are two lodge houses.

Bonaly village was destroyed by Lord Cockburn when he decided to make Bonaly his home. Although this sounds rather drastic, the community at Bonaly was already dispersing before his arrival. In March 1811 he married and set up home at Bonaly in a derelict farmhouse, which had been built around 1650. Cockburn extended the farmhouse, and a turreted library wing was added in 1888. A statue of Shakespeare, salvaged from the demolition of Shakespeare Square in the centre of Edinburgh, stands in the garden. Bonaly Tower has now been converted into flats.

Edinburgh's Fever Hospital (today's City Hospital) was built on land bought from Colinton Mains Farm. King Edward VII and Queen Alexandra officially opened it on 13 May 1903. Strict isolation was maintained for patients. Each one was provided with a reference number, and daily reports were issued in the local newspapers alongside these codes, thus protecting patients' identities. Relatives were able to visit if summoned in the newspaper.

In 1905 news spread that the War Department intended to build a cavalry and infantry barracks to the south of Colinton Road, and the new Redford Barracks, built between 1909 and 1915, were finished in time to accommodate soldiers training to fight in the First World War. In 1913 an additional 730 acres of land was acquired at Dreghorn at a cost of £35,000, although the building of more barracks there didn't begin until 1938.

During the building work, a specially constructed rail link was developed to bring materials from Slateford to the site of Redford Barracks. Like those at Dreghorn, the barracks were named after the estate their land had previously formed part of. The stables are in the background.

The writing room at the Royal Soliders Home, Colinton, was described by one soldier as a 'Godsend' because of the peace and quiet. He also mentioned a typical menu in the restaurant as consisting of: Rissole & Mash, 6d; Pie & Chips, 5d; Sausage & Mash, 6d; Liver & Onions, 7d; Tea, 1d a cup; and Minerals, 3d a glass.

Soldiers marching over the bridge from the station towards Redford Barracks. The British Linen Bank, now the Royal Bank of Scotland, is to the right. Colinton and the army barracks have had a long association, with soldiers leaving a church service early after being told from the pulpit of the start of the Second World War; children being evacuated by train to East Calder because of the proximity of the barracks and the chance of air raids; a memorial to the fallen of both World Wars within the church; and good wishes being offered by the congregation when the King's Own Scottish Borderers left for the Gulf War. The house in the centre of the picture was the County Roadman's house. At one stage Colinton man William Robertson lived upstairs, while the lower floor was occupied by Peter Stenhouse of Juniper Green.